The Civilization Library

Published in the United States by
Gloucester Press in 1978

Designed by David Cook and
Associates and produced
by the Archon Press Ltd
28 Percy Street
London W1P 9FF

First published in
Great Britain 1977 by
Hamish Hamilton
Children's Books Ltd
90 Great Russell Street
London WC1B 3PT

Printed in Italy
by Alfieri & Lacroix

Library of Congress Cataloging in Publication Data

Boase, Wendy.
  Ancient Egypt.

  (The Civilization library)
  Includes index.
  SUMMARY: Discusses the history, rulers, and
culture of ancient Egypt.
  1. Egypt—Civilization—To-332 B.C.—Juvenile
literature. [1. Egypt—Civilization—To-332 B.C.]
I. McBride, Angus. II. Thomas, Eric. III. Title.
DT61.B58 1978   923'.01   77–10779
ISBN 0–531–01402–9

THE CIVILIZATION LIBRARY

ANCIENT EGYPT

Wendy Boase

Special Editorial Consultant
W. V. Davies,
Assistant Keeper of Egyptology,
The British Museum, London

Illustrated by
Angus McBride, Eric Thomas

Gloucester Press | New York | 1978

The kingdom of Egypt

Faces of the God-Kings
Many rulers left their portraits in stone. From the top of the picture we see: Zoser of the Old Kingdom; Khufu (or Cheops), builder of the Great Pyramid; and Amenemhet III. The next three were rulers of the New Kingdom: Queen Hatshepsut; her warrior stepson Thutmose III; and Ramses II, who reigned for 67 years.

As it runs through the barren North African desert, the Nile creates a narrow strip of fertile land—the country of Egypt. This is a long, narrow land, protected by rocky deserts on both sides, with a great river providing a highway from one end to the other. Here was the setting for one of the most enduring civilizations of the ancient world—lasting over 3,000 years.

The first people to live in the Nile valley were prehistoric hunters driven north from drought-parched central Africa. They settled in small farming communities. Eventually, two separate kingdoms developed—Upper Egypt (in the south) and Lower Egypt (in the north).

It is said that the two kingdoms were united by King Narmer (or Menes) of Upper Egypt. An ancient carved palette (a slate used for mixing cosmetics) shows Narmer triumphant over Lower Egypt. He wears the crown of Lower Egypt, and has ten headless bodies at his feet.

Egypt's history is divided into a number of periods within which the dynasties, or ruling families, of kings are grouped. Narmer was the first king of the First Dynasty.

A time of prosperity began with the Fourth Dynasty, in the period called the Old Kingdom. At this time the pyramids, the tombs of the kings, were built—the first great monuments to Egyptian power and skill. But the last rulers of the Old Kingdom were weak and lost power. This led to over 200 years of chaos known as the First Intermediate period. The princes of Thebes emerged as rulers after the time of war and unrest.

The Middle Kingdom rulers of the Eleventh and Twelfth Dynasties sent out trading and military expeditions and extended Egypt's southern borders. But this prosperity was destroyed by weak kings of the next two dynasties. The Second Intermediate period was one of Egypt's darkest times. The country was invaded by the Hyksos, warlike nomads from the east, who ruled for 200 years.

Again the rulers of Thebes came forward and drove out the invaders. The 400-year span of the New Kingdom that followed was the most splendid era. But the glory faded. In the Late Dynastic period the country was ruled by a series of foreigners. Cleopatra was the last ruler of the dynasty founded by Ptolemy, Alexander the Great's general. With her death Egypt became a province of Rome.

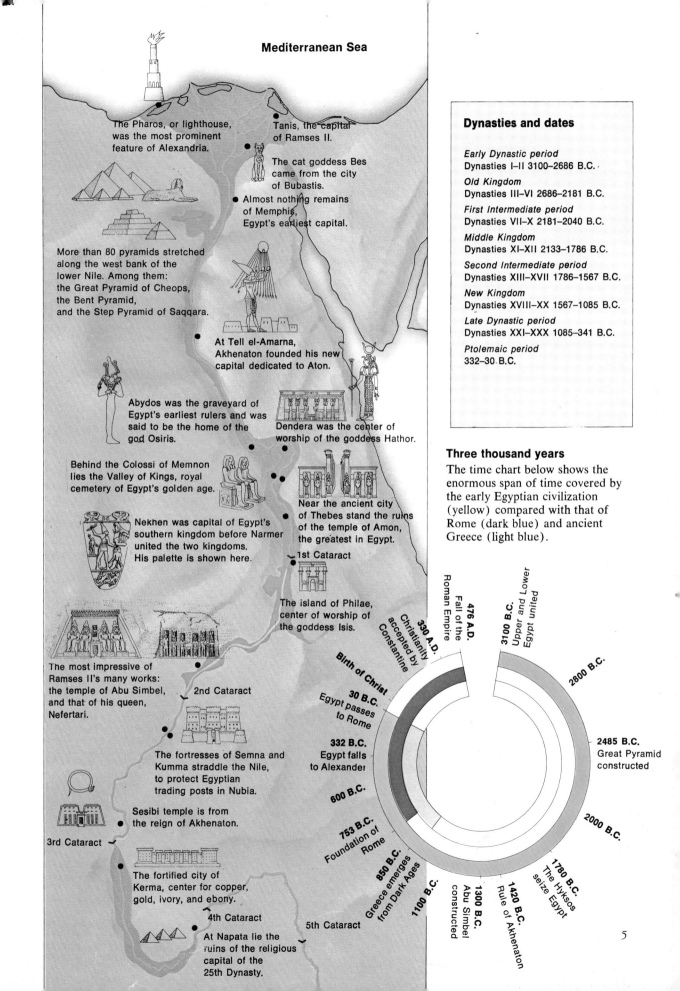

Mediterranean Sea

The Pharos, or lighthouse, was the most prominent feature of Alexandria.

Tanis, the capital of Ramses II.

The cat goddess Bes came from the city of Bubastis.

Almost nothing remains of Memphis, Egypt's earliest capital.

More than 80 pyramids stretched along the west bank of the lower Nile. Among them: the Great Pyramid of Cheops, the Bent Pyramid, and the Step Pyramid of Saqqara.

At Tell el-Amarna, Akhenaton founded his new capital dedicated to Aton.

Abydos was the graveyard of Egypt's earliest rulers and was said to be the home of the god Osiris.

Dendera was the center of worship of the goddess Hathor.

Behind the Colossi of Memnon lies the Valley of Kings, royal cemetery of Egypt's golden age.

Near the ancient city of Thebes stand the ruins of the temple of Amon, the greatest in Egypt.

Nekhen was capital of Egypt's southern kingdom before Narmer united the two kingdoms. His palette is shown here.

1st Cataract

The island of Philae, center of worship of the goddess Isis.

The most impressive of Ramses II's many works: the temple of Abu Simbel, and that of his queen, Nefertari.

2nd Cataract

The fortresses of Semna and Kumma straddle the Nile, to protect Egyptian trading posts in Nubia.

Sesibi temple is from the reign of Akhenaton.

3rd Cataract

The fortified city of Kerma, center for copper, gold, ivory, and ebony.

4th Cataract

5th Cataract

At Napata lie the ruins of the religious capital of the 25th Dynasty.

Dynasties and dates

Early Dynastic period
Dynasties I–II 3100–2686 B.C.

Old Kingdom
Dynasties III–VI 2686–2181 B.C.

First Intermediate period
Dynasties VII–X 2181–2040 B.C.

Middle Kingdom
Dynasties XI–XII 2133–1786 B.C.

Second Intermediate period
Dynasties XIII–XVII 1786–1567 B.C.

New Kingdom
Dynasties XVIII–XX 1567–1085 B.C.

Late Dynastic period
Dynasties XXI–XXX 1085–341 B.C.

Ptolemaic period
332–30 B.C.

Three thousand years

The time chart below shows the enormous span of time covered by the early Egyptian civilization (yellow) compared with that of Rome (dark blue) and ancient Greece (light blue).

476 A.D. Fall of the Roman Empire

330 A.D. Christianity accepted by Constantine

Birth of Christ

30 B.C. Egypt passes to Rome

332 B.C. Egypt falls to Alexander

600 B.C.

753 B.C. Foundation of Rome

850 B.C. Greece emerges from Dark Ages

1100 B.C.

1300 B.C. Abu Simbel constructed

1420 B.C. Rule of Akhenaton

1780 B.C. The Hyksos seize Egypt

2000 B.C.

2485 B.C. Great Pyramid constructed

2800 B.C.

3100 B.C. Upper and Lower Egypt united

Building an empire

Symbols of royal power
In early times each province of Egypt had its own god, usually shown as an animal. The tall, white crown of Upper Egypt had a cobra's head on it, while the red crown of Lower Egypt bore a vulture. When the two kingdoms were united, the pharaohs of the two lands each wore a red and white crown, with both animals.

To the Egyptians, the pharaoh was the representative on earth of the sun god, Amon, and all the land and people belonged to him. Ceremonies and rituals were reminders of his godlike power.

Some of the greatest pharaohs ruled during the New Kingdom. Thutmose I, of the Eighteenth Dynasty, fought a campaign in Nubia and extended the southern border as far as the third cataract (rapids) on the Nile.

Another outstanding pharaoh of the same dynasty was Queen Hatshepsut, widow of Thutmose II and stepmother of Thutmose III. Like the male pharaohs she claimed divine birth, and statues show her wearing the double crown and even the ceremonial royal beard.

After Hatshepsut's death, her stepson removed her name and image from buildings and monuments. Then, for almost every spring of his rule, he sent military expeditions to Asia to subdue rebellious lands and demand tribute. With this treasure, he built grand halls and gateways to honor Amon, god of Thebes, at Karnak.

The best-known pharaoh of the Nineteenth Dynasty is Ramses II, "the Great." His long reign (over 60 years) began with almost 20 years of continuous war against the Hittites. After a decisive battle at Kadesh, in Syria, peace was established and Ramses devoted himself to building projects like the temple at Abu Simbel.

Queen Hatshepsut's temple

An avenue of sphinxes once led
to the shining limestone temple
beneath the cliffs at Deir
el-Bahri. Scenes from the queen's
life decorate the walls.
Hatshepsut built the temple
to honor Amon-Re, the sun god.

Moving a colossus

Giant statues, or colossi, of the
New Kingdom pharaohs show their
power, and their pride. Over
170 laborers, using sledges,
levers, and ropes, were needed to
move a 60-ton statue.

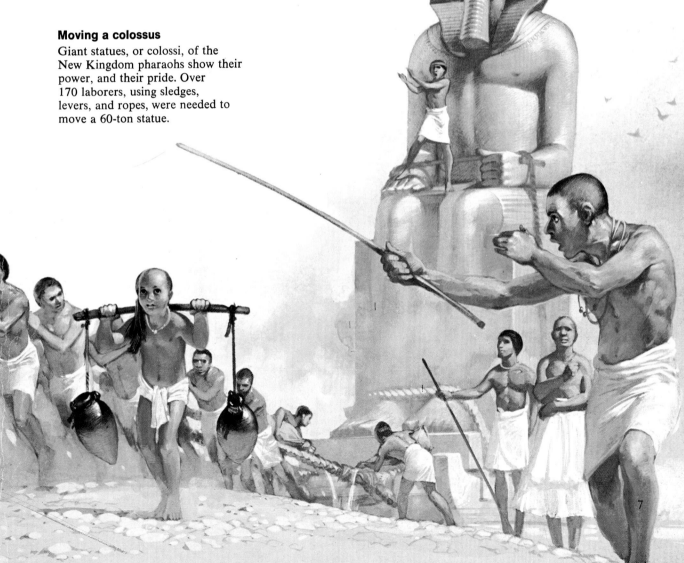

The land of Egypt

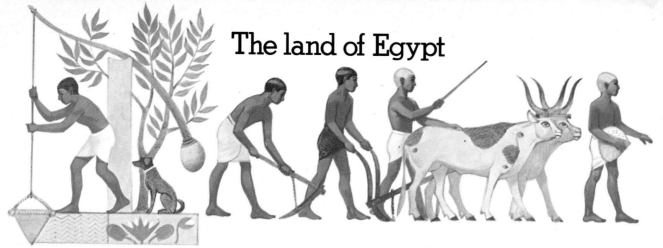

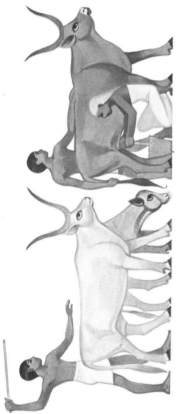

The splendid civilization of ancient Egypt was based on a prosperous farming economy. Along the length of the Nile the land blossomed with wheat, barley, fruit, vegetables, and herd animals. The rich, dark soil led the Egyptians to call their country *Kemet,* "the black land."

The farming year was divided into three seasons by the behavior of the Nile. The "inundation" (flooding) lasted from June until September: the Nile overflowed its banks and flooded the fields. The peasants worked on the king's building projects, using the floodwaters to float huge stone blocks on rafts. In the next season, October to February, the water went down leaving a layer of rich silt on the fields. The peasants sowed crops and dug irrigation ditches. In the drought season, March to May, they harvested crops and the wild papyrus reed that was used to make paper, boats, baskets, and ropes.

There were sometimes bad years, when the cycle of flood and drought was broken and the crops failed. But food could be stored for a bad year—as Joseph in the Bible story advised his pharaoh to do after his dream of "seven lean years." Irrigation systems helped save some crops too.

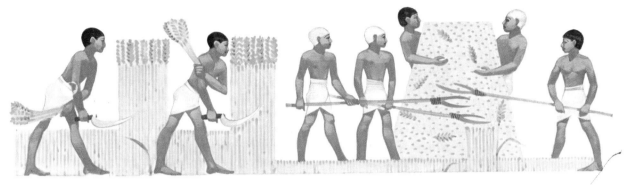

The fertile Delta

At the end of a 4,000-mile journey, the ancient Nile emptied into the Mediterranean by seven separate waterways, making lower Egypt—the Delta—the most fertile area in the country. Egyptians raised cattle (A), pigs (B), and goats (C). Barley (D), grapes (E), and date palms (F) were grown, and also flax (G) for linen and sesame plants (H) for oil. Papyrus (I) grew wild and there were many birds in the marshes—cranes, geese, and ducks.

The farmer's year

This frieze, or series of pictures, is like those that decorate temples and tombs. It shows the busy life of a farming people. First the ground is broken for planting by hand or with cattle-drawn ploughs. Grain is planted. The harvest is cut with sickles and stacked with forks. Donkeys carry grain to be threshed. Papyrus reeds are gathered, and the geese who live among them are driven home to be fattened. Honey is collected from a hive. Grapes are picked and pressed for their juice. Cattle, which are also used for meat, are milked. A peasant uses a shadoof, a bucket on a pole, to fill the irrigation ditches. The bucket is lowered into the Nile; a heavy weight on the other end of the pole raises it again, filled with water.

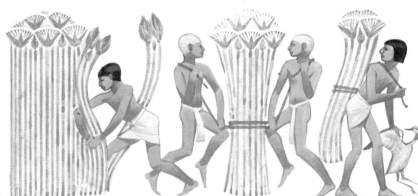

The craft of war

Prisoners of war

Foreign captives were tied and branded as slaves. They included Libyans, Nubians, the Hittites, Syrians, and Mitanni of Asia, Semites from Palestine, and later, the Sea Peoples from across the Mediterranean.

The civilization of ancient Egypt was not based on military strength and conquest, although there were some noted battles. Scenes on tombs from the Old Kingdom show the Egyptians had soldiers, and knew something about warfare and armor. But they did not have a national army. In an emergency, the governors of the provinces called up armies from among their peasants. The foot soldiers fought almost naked, with bronze- or copper-tipped spears, small axes, and bows.

The rulers of the Middle Kingdom ended the old system of raising local armies—which local leaders could use against each other—and set up a trained, central army under their own command. This new Egyptian army was stronger, but was still no match for the Hyksos. In 1786 B.C. these Asiatic warriors swept into the Nile valley in horse-drawn chariots, armed with bronze swords and powerful bows. They controlled Egypt for about 200 years, until the Egyptians learned to use the horses, chariots, and weapons of their enemy and drove the foreigners out.

The war machine

The chariots that carried the pharaohs into battle were light and strong. They could turn quickly in a small space.

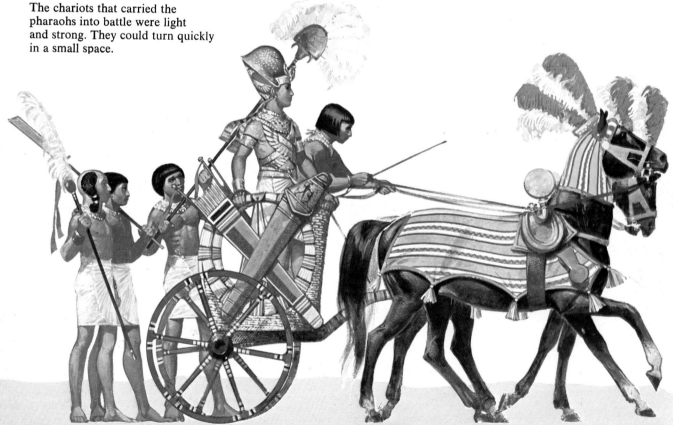

The New Kingdom pharaohs planned conquests against neighboring lands that were threatening. The pharaoh led his army, sometimes accompanied by a trained lion. The soldiers were professional, and had body armor and new weapons. The archers had strong bows and arrows, while other soldiers were armed with metal-tipped spears, axes, bronze daggers, and scimitars (curved swords copied from the Syrians). Chariots, each carrying a driver and an archer, raced past the enemy, shooting into their ranks.

In the New Kingdom period, Egyptian troops won a famous sea battle in the Mediterranean. Ramses III met a fleet of ships raised by the Sea Peoples in 1190 B.C. Their vessels were swamped as a storm of arrows came from Ramses' solid wall of warships.

The Egyptian empire of the New Kingdom was vast. Nubia, the land to the south, was held the tightest. An Egyptian viceroy ruled, and a 100-mile-long chain of forts guarded the road to the Nubian gold mines and protected Egypt from the warlike people of Kush, farther south.

Frontier strongholds
Egyptian forts had thick walls and massive towers of masonry and mud brick. Strong gates and a wide ditch protected them from attack.

A military review
Middle Kingdom foot soldiers were armed with bows and arrows, spears, slings, and axes. They carried shields made of bull's hide.

Shipping and trade

Papyrus boat
This was made of bundles
of papyrus reeds tied together.

The world's oldest picture of a boat comes from Egypt. The Egyptians—living on the banks of the Nile—used water transport more than any other kind. Prehistoric Egyptians paddled down the river on papyrus rafts. As early as 3000 B.C., they built wooden ships with sails. Oars were used on the river, but in the narrow canals the crews walked alongside the water and pulled their boats by ropes.

At the height of the Egyptian empire, the Nile was like a busy highway: flimsy reed boats and tiny ferries jostled with huge cargo ships, 200-foot long barges, and sleek galleys. Magnificent vessels carried the images of gods at festivals.

The Egyptians sailed out to the open sea early. The Old Kingdom pharaoh Sahure sent eight armed ships across the Mediterranean to attack Syria. Sneferu opened trade with Lebanon when he sent forty ships to buy wood.

Egyptian power was at its peak in the New Kingdom. Sea and land trading routes were always busy. Since there was no money (coins were not used until the 4th century B.C.), Egypt bartered linen, papyrus, and other materials for foreign goods. They traded gold from Nubia for African ivory and animal skins. Horses, cattle, silver, bronze, and rare woods were brought in from Asia, chariots from Syria, and jewelry from Babylon.

Trading with the land of Punt
Queen Hatshepsut sent a trading expedition to the land of Punt. Pictures on the walls of her temple at Deir el-Bahri tell the story of the expedition. Five galleys sailed down the Red Sea, carrying necklaces, daggers, and hatchets. They returned filled with wood, ivory, trees, animal skins, and even a live panther. Trading vessels like this one had special equipment for loading heavy cargo like timber.

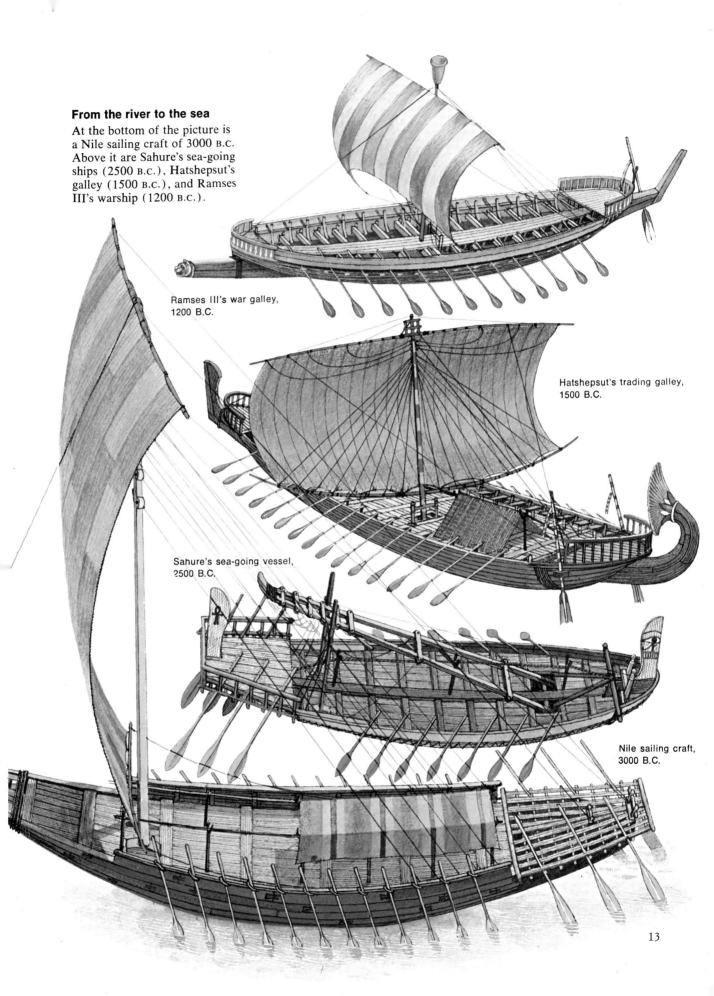

From the river to the sea

At the bottom of the picture is
a Nile sailing craft of 3000 B.C.
Above it are Sahure's sea-going
ships (2500 B.C.), Hatshepsut's
galley (1500 B.C.), and Ramses
III's warship (1200 B.C.).

Ramses III's war galley,
1200 B.C.

Hatshepsut's trading galley,
1500 B.C.

Sahure's sea-going vessel,
2500 B.C.

Nile sailing craft,
3000 B.C.

13

Society and the law

Maat
The goddess Maat, whose symbol was an ostrich feather, stood for world order, truth, and justice. To the pharaohs, living by *maat* meant ruling justly; to the peasants, it meant working honestly.

The Egyptians believed the gods created the world and everything in it following a principle of truth, justice, and order they called *maat*. Since the world was just as the gods wanted, the people did not expect change, or try to change things themselves; and their society changed little in 3000 years. In art, as in other areas, everything was done in a fixed way. Figures on tombs from the New Kingdom are carved in the same style as those on the palette of Narmer, the first king.

The pharaoh personified *maat,* and his task was to establish *maat* instead of disorder. In the Middle Kingdom, as Egypt grew more powerful, the pharaohs appointed officials to help govern. They were often scribes or clerks, for many records were kept—especially of taxes which were collected in real goods, like corn or animals. New Kingdom pharaohs appointed a chief official, called a vizier.

The vizier and other officials, and the priests and nobles, were the upper class of society. Below were scribes, soldiers, craftsmen, laborers, slaves, and peasants. The peasants' children remained peasants; those of craftsmen were trained in crafts; the sons of nobles inherited their positions. But the society was not all rigid. Ability to read and write was the best way to advance, but soldiers too could sometimes reach higher positions. And, unlike most ancient civilizations, Egyptian society gave women and slaves some legal rights—for example, they could own property.

A court of law
The trial scene (right) shows village chiefs accused of not collecting taxes properly. The vizier, the pharaoh's chief minister, acts as judge. The scribes record everything that happens. Sometimes special scribes helped defendants prepare their cases. The vizier read written evidence, heard witnesses, and then announced his verdict. If found guilty, the defendant could be whipped or imprisoned. The stone carving (bottom left) shows defendants kneeling before the court to beg for mercy.

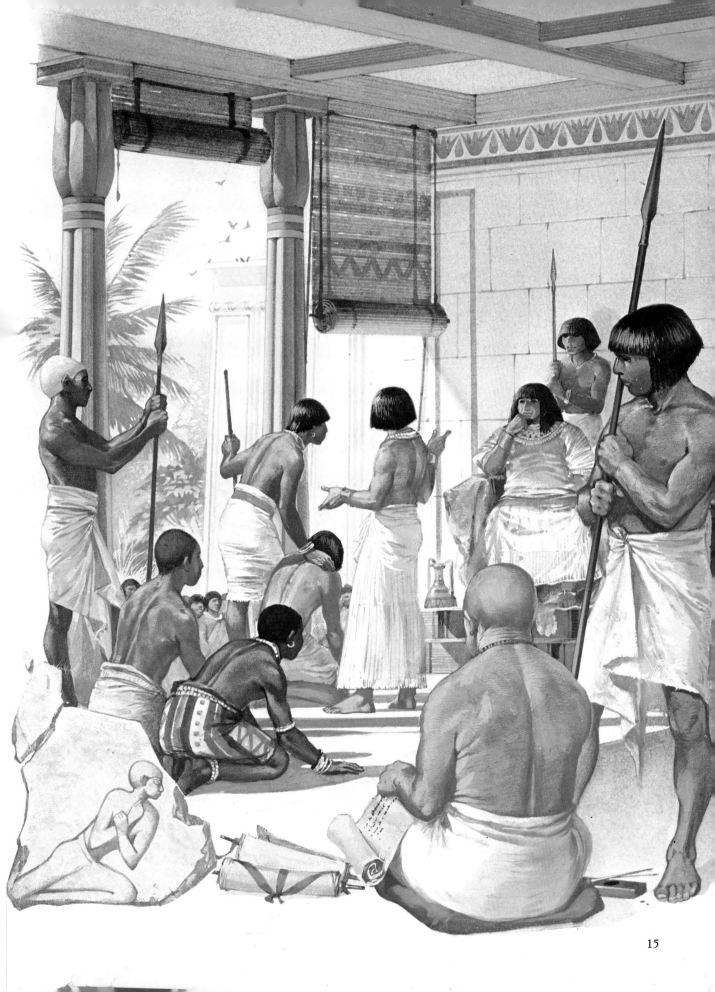

15

The gods

Before the kingdom of Egypt was united, it consisted of a number of tribal settlements, each with its own divinity that gradually developed into a local god. These earliest gods, like those of most prehistoric peoples, were associated with natural forces—the sun, the wind, the rise and fall of the Nile. Many had animal qualities such as the fierceness of a lion, the strength of a bull, and, at first, all the gods had animal forms.

In time, the gods were given human forms, and sometimes the influence of one god spread beyond a local area. Amon, god of Thebes, was originally shown as a ram or goose. As Thebes became the capital city, Amon grew in importance. By the time of the New Kingdom, Amon was king of the gods and great temples to him were built at Karnak. The only trace of his animal origin were two feathers worn at the back of the head in his statues.

Gradually, Amon was woven into the myths of Re, or Ra, the sun god. The two gods were combined, and were worshipped as one god, Amon-Re. Later gods—Osiris, god of the dead, and his sister-wife Isis, the mother goddess —were also brought into the family of the older gods.

Neith of Sais

Ptah of Memphis

Re

Anubis

Sebek

Horus of Edfu

Shu

Isis

Uachet of Buto

Horus the child

Amon of Thebes

The creation of the world

Egyptians pictured the sky as a star-covered goddess, Nut, and the earth as her husband-brother, Geb. At first Geb and Nut lived together. But Re, the sun god, ordered them to be separated. Their father, Shu, caused a great wind to lift Nut's body, and so created space between them. Shu became god of air—between Nut, the sky, and Geb, the earth, below. Each day Re, the sun, traveled across the arc of Nut's body. At night the sky goddess descended to her husband, thus creating darkness. Geb and Nut were the parents of Osiris, Isis, and Set. Osiris was killed by his jealous brother, Set. But Isis, his sister-wife, performed the special rites to preserve his body and thus gave him the power to live again. The Egyptians believed they too could live after death by preserving their bodies.

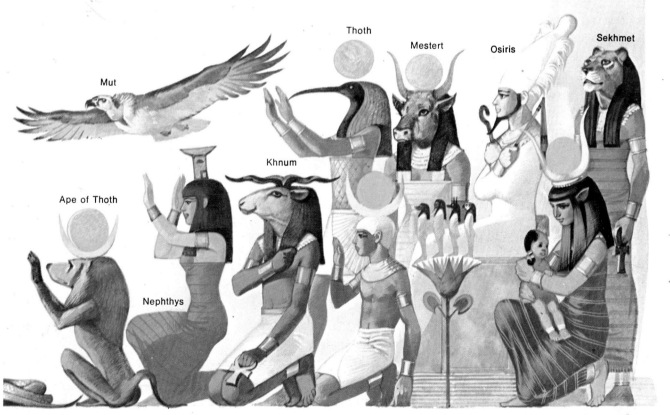

Mut

Thoth

Mestert

Osiris

Sekhmet

Ape of Thoth

Khnum

Nephthys

Khonsu Sons of Horus Hathor

Temples and priests

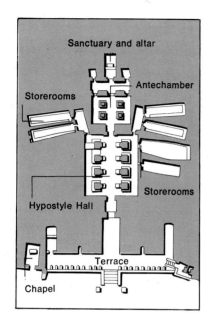

Abu Simbel

This mighty temple, cut out of a sandstone cliff, was dedicated by its builder, Ramses II, to the sun god, Re. It was designed for the worship of the sun at dawn. A row of baboons was carved across the top of the front of the temple. They were sacred to the god of wisdom and to the rising sun. Four huge, painted statues of the pharaoh, each 65 feet high, guarded the entrance.

Egyptian temples were built to honor the gods and to record the deeds of the pharaohs who hoped to join the gods after death. Every ruler felt he or she should build a temple, or add shrines or statues to those already built. As certain gods grew in importance, the priests who served in their temples became more powerful.

In the New Kingdom the mightiest god was Amon, patron of Thebes. Generations of pharaohs added to a temple at Karnak that was dedicated to him. It grew from a small shrine into the greatest temple ever built. Ramses II, the most ambitious builder of all the pharaohs, added the great Hypostyle Hall. (The name comes from a Greek word meaning "to rest on pillars.") The hall's roof was supported by 134 columns, each showing scenes of the pharaoh worshiping Amon.

At Abu Simbel, Ramses built two more temples. The sanctuary of the larger is cut 60 yards into the rock. Only twice a year—on February 23 and October 23—do the sun's rays reach the huge statues of Ramses and the gods inside.

The vast temples were only part of an enormous area that included houses for the priests, a school, storerooms, and workshops. Priests had many duties. Some performed daily rituals in the dead pharaoh's temples. Others spent every fourth month serving the gods in their special temples. Only a few chosen priests were allowed inside the temple. Each day they entered the sanctuary and the high priest broke the clay seal on the doors of the shrine where the god's statue was kept. A ritual of prayers and bathing and dressing the statue was performed. It was then resealed in the sanctuary with an offering of food and drink.

19

A revolutionary pharaoh

In the 14th century B.C., the power of the priests and the old religion was challenged by a strange and fascinating pharaoh. Amenhotep IV (or Amenophis) was a revolutionary ruler; he caused great changes in many areas of life. He introduced a new religion and his reign saw the founding of a new capital city, and the creation of a very different art style.

For almost 2,000 years, Egyptians had prayed to a great variety of gods. Monotheism, the worship of one god, had never existed. The new pharaoh now chose Aton to be honored above all gods. The Aton was the sun's disk—the visible part of the sun that sends its beams to earth, the source of light and life.

To honor his god, Amenhotep took the name Akhenaton ("he who serves Aton") and his queen, the beautiful Nefertiti, adopted Nefer-neferu-Aton ("fair is the goodness of Aton"). Akhenaton left Thebes, the city of Amon, to build a new capital dedicated to Aton. Nearly 300 miles north, near the modern village of Tell el-Amarna, Akhetaton was built, with lakes, gardens, painted walks, royal temples, and an immense palace facing the Nile. The buildings were decorated with scenes of everyday life and portraits of people—even the pharaoh—in realistic poses.

In the Amarna style (from Tell el-Amarna), the family

Portrait of a pharaoh
The statue below shows the defects Akhenaton allowed his sculptors to portray. These may have been caused by a gland disorder.

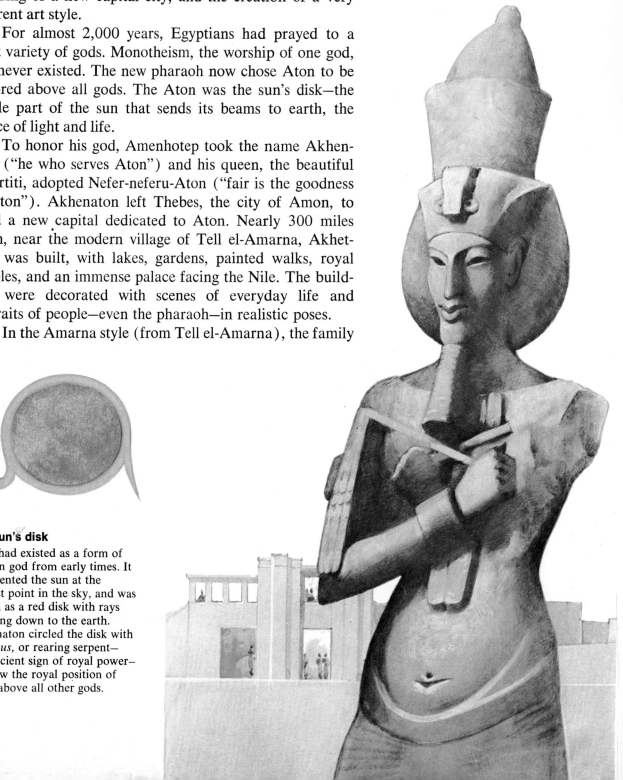

The sun's disk
Aton had existed as a form of the sun god from early times. It represented the sun at the highest point in the sky, and was shown as a red disk with rays reaching down to the earth. Akhenaton circled the disk with a *uraeus,* or rearing serpent—the ancient sign of royal power—to show the royal position of Aton above all other gods.

life of the palace was shown in a natural manner: Nefertiti with a child on her knee, Akhenaton and his queen holding hands, or kissing their daughters. Akhenaton's appearance is surprising. He is shown with a long, thin head, drooping shoulders, a round belly, and fat thighs. This new naturalism in style and subject was a startling change.

But the Amarna period was only a brief flicker in the long history of Egyptian civilization. When Akhenaton died, his successor, Tutankhamon, returned to Thebes and to the old religion and the old art.

The beautiful Nefertiti

Paintings found in the ruins of the palace of Akhetaton include many portrait groups of Nefertiti playing with her six daughters. One daughter became the wife of Tutankhamon.

The city of Aton

Constructed in record time, and abandoned equally quickly when its founder died, Akhetaton stretched for eight miles along the Nile.
At the center was a complex of palaces and temples, all revolving around the enormous Temple of the Sun's Disk.

Life and leisure

Although Egyptian art was very formal (except for the Amarna period), there were many human touches that show everyday activities. Tomb paintings show hunting scenes, feasts, parties, games, and dancing: all the activities the wealthy Egyptians hoped to continue after death in the next world.

Only the upper classes—nobles, important soldiers, and officials—lived this well. Their large estates were managed by scribes who kept careful records of the crops and animals. Many servants worked in the vineyards, picking grapes and treading them for wine. They looked after the herds of cattle, goats, and antelope. The indoor servants cooked, brewed beer, laundered, wove linen, and served at table.

The family could relax in the garden of their house. Girls practiced dancing and played. When not studying, boys wrestled or played tug-of-war. The adults enjoyed board or dice games. A popular sport was hunting on the banks of the Nile with throwing sticks.

Feasts were very popular. Long tables were piled with meat, game, fruit, bread and pastries, and huge amounts of wine and beer, for the Egyptians enjoyed drinking.

Both men and women wore eye makeup, and women also placed cones of greasy incense on their heads so that, as the feast continued, the melting grease perfumed their hair. Guests were entertained by singers, dancing girls, the music of harps and flutes, and by dwarfs and acrobats who performed tricks.

A noble's estate

Surrounded by high walls and formal gardens, a rich family's country residence was like a well-planned village. Kitchens, workshops, servants' quarters, storerooms, grain silos, and sheds for animals were separated from the main building. In the spacious mud-brick house, a large living area (with a ceiling resting on columns) led to the main bedroom, toilets, and bathrooms. Stairs led to the roof.

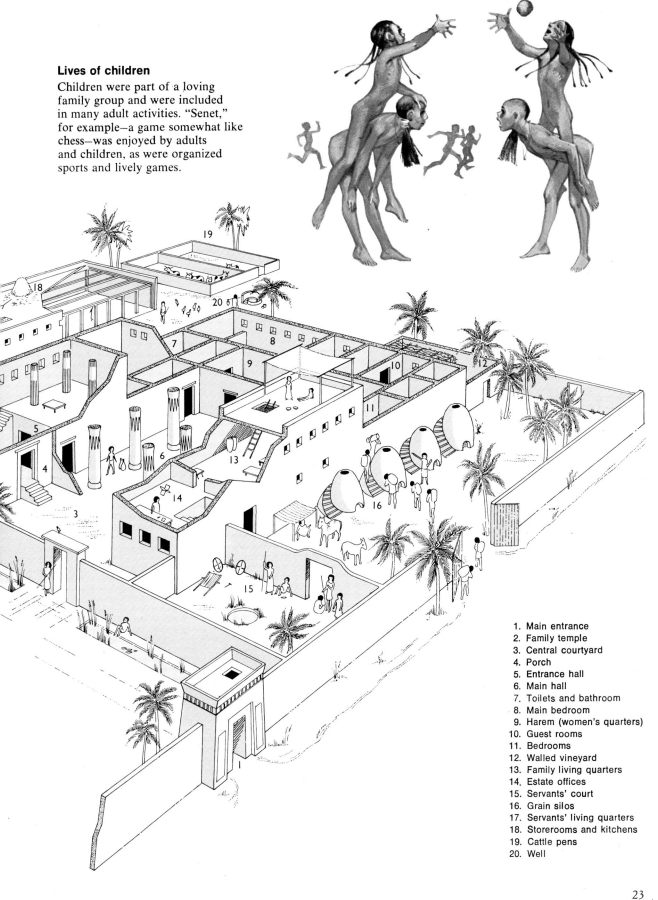

Lives of children

Children were part of a loving
family group and were included
in many adult activities. "Senet,"
for example—a game somewhat like
chess—was enjoyed by adults
and children, as were organized
sports and lively games.

1. Main entrance
2. Family temple
3. Central courtyard
4. Porch
5. Entrance hall
6. Main hall
7. Toilets and bathroom
8. Main bedroom
9. Harem (women's quarters)
10. Guest rooms
11. Bedrooms
12. Walled vineyard
13. Family living quarters
14. Estate offices
15. Servants' court
16. Grain silos
17. Servants' living quarters
18. Storerooms and kitchens
19. Cattle pens
20. Well

23

Education and ambition

Schools for scribes

A New Kingdom scribe studied for about 12 years to learn the more than 700 hieroglyphs used at the time. From the age of 5, boys spent hours copying individual signs, as well as long pieces. Older pupils learned letter-writing, bookkeeping, mathematics, and astronomy—the subjects they would need in their careers.

Painted wooden statue of a New Kingdom scribe

The beginner's materials

Only fully trained scribes wrote on the beautiful paper made from papyrus. Students practiced hieroglyphs on chips of pottery or stone, or on wooden tablets. They used reed pens or brushes.

The work of the scribe in ancient Egypt was like work in a modern office: making reports, writing letters, recording events, and keeping accounts. But because he could read and write, the scribe was an important person and could reach a high position.

At school, boys were taught reading, writing, and mathematics to prepare them for careers as government officials, priests, or administrators for wealthy families. Handwriting and composition were learned by copying models.

A scribe might first work at calculating land areas or numbers of stones quarried, or at recording taxes. He might work for a wealthy family, for the army, or among government officials or priests. If ambitious, he could rise to a powerful office, like chief of public works, royal architect, or even governor of a province.

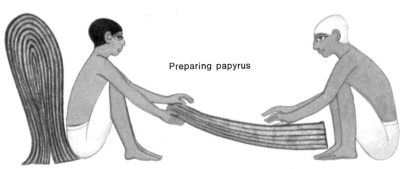

Preparing papyrus

The slab of basalt, found near Rosetta in 1799, showed three scripts—hieroglyphic (A), demotic (B), and Greek (C). Groups of ringed hieroglyphs

A

(cartouches) were royal names and could be matched with the Greek names of the rulers. Champollion identified the symbols and sounds (*p,o,l*) that occur in the names of

B

Ptolemy and Cleopatra, and worked out the other letters by their positions. At last the words on the Rosetta Stone could be read.

ΠΤΟΛΕΜΑΙΟΣ

C

The professional scribe wrote on clay tablets or papyrus scrolls. The scrolls were made by first cutting thin strips of pith, the spongy center of a papyrus reed. These were put in layers across a stone. They were beaten with wooden mallets until the natural juice, acting like glue, bound them together. Single sheets were then pasted into a long roll.

The Egyptians had learned to make paper in the First Dynasty, and their written language dates from this time. Hieroglyphs, or miniature pictures, sometimes stand for a whole word or idea, and are called ideograms. The word for house ⊐ looks like an outline of a house. Other hieroglyphs have a phonetic, or sound, value and are called phonograms. The owl 𓅓 stands for the sound *m* and the snake ⌒ for *f*. There were hundreds of signs and they could be written as the scribe pleased—from left to right, right to left, or in columns. Hieroglyphs continued to be used for sacred writing, but a system called hieratic was developed for everyday use. Simple strokes replaced the symbols. Much later, in 700 B.C., demotic, or popular, script was developed.

By the 4th century A.D., the meaning of the hieroglyphs had been lost. It was not until 1822 that Jean François Champollion, a French scholar, worked out the hieroglyphs on the Rosetta Stone and opened the secrets of ancient Egypt.

Scribes at work

Preparing for the afterlife

Ancient Egyptians believed the land of the dead would be like the Nile valley. After death, they would live there with the gods in eternal happiness. First, only royalty was thought to enjoy the afterlife. By the New Kingdom, nobles and even commoners expected it too.

If a person's spirit or *ka* was to survive, the body had to be preserved as a mummy through embalming. The embalmer removed the brain and contents of the abdomen and chest (except for the heart, which would be needed for judgment in the afterlife). The body was washed with wine and spices, and covered with salts for up to 70 days to dry. The organs were preserved in four containers called

Canopic Jars. The body was packed with linen and spices, rubbed with oil or wine, and coated with resin. It was wrapped in strips of linen. Amulets (charms) like the ankh, symbol of life, were put in the linen. Priests and family performed ceremonies that would restore the body to life. Then the mummy was carried to the tomb in a coffin.

Because the next world was a mirror reflection of this one, the dead were buried with clothes, furniture, and models of servants. The *ka* could survive only if it had food (which was left daily or ensured by prayers) and a home—the tomb. Tomb robbers were feared since they destroyed the dead's hope of eternal life.

Animals honored in death
Beasts associated with the gods were often mummified. The scarab beetle, crocodile, and cat were embalmed and buried with humans or in their own cemeteries.

A ritual farewell
The mummy is held up while the family and priests perform the Opening of the Mouth ceremony. This was believed to give the dead person the power to breathe.

Travel in the next world
Model boats like those that carried the dead pharaohs across the Nile were often put in the tomb.

Judgment of the gods
A feather, symbol of *maat,* or truth, is weighed against the dead person's heart. Several gods watch as the balance is presented to Osiris for his verdict.

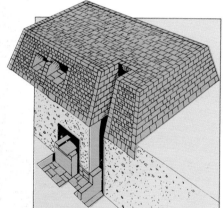

The mastabas

These were rectangular tombs of mud brick. Some were large enough to have room for storage as well as bodies.

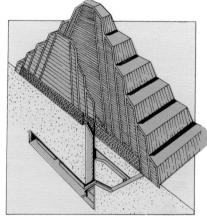

The step pyramid at Saqqara

The world's oldest stone building, raised by the architect Imhotep for King Zoser. Imhotep became famous for his skill in building and medicine, and was later worshiped as a god.

The Mountains of Pharaoh

The Arabs called the pyramids "the Mountains of Pharaoh." To the Egyptians, they were vast tombs, built to ensure a glorious afterlife for the rulers. There are about 80 pyramids, along the edge of the Nile.

Until the Third Dynasty, all buildings were of mud brick. Then King Zoser built a step pyramid of stone, instead of the usual mastaba (the earth-covered tomb) of his ancestors. A century later, the ruler Cheops (or Khufu) built the largest of the true pyramids—the Great Pyramid of Giza.

At Giza, gangs of workers used copper chisels and saws to cut stones from cliffs. They used levers to get the stones on sledges to be hauled to the building site. Granite blocks weighing over 15 tons were floated down the Nile from Aswan, about 500 miles away. Masons laid a core of solid masonry, and then chambers and passages were tunneled deep into it. As the pyramid rose, stone blocks were dragged up ramps and levered into position on a layer of mortar. Finally, the pyramid was faced (covered) with polished limestone or granite, and the halls inside it were decorated with scenes of the pharaoh's life.

Guardian of the dead
The Great Sphinx, crouched in the sand at Giza, has guarded the pyramids for 46 centuries.

Rediscovery

Tutankhamon

Nearly 1000 years before the pharaoh Tutankhamon was buried in the Valley of the Kings, all the great pyramids there had already been broken into and robbed. Most of the tombs at Thebes were entered too. Only Tutankhamon's escaped.
The young ruler was buried with incredible treasures: golden animals, statues, magnificent furniture, and weapons. In one chamber the mummified body of Tutankhamon, undisturbed for 3000 years, lay in a coffin of solid gold. Over his head was this portrait mask of beaten gold, inlaid with blue glass and lapis lazuli, a semiprecious stone. But Tutankhamon was an unimportant king who died at about 18, and had ruled for only 9 years. The wealth of the powerful New Kingdom pharaohs must have been truly unbelievable.

The civilization of ancient Egypt died 2000 years ago, but along the banks of the Nile, its people left a record of their lives, their religion, and their achievements. Many of their monuments were long ago plundered by other builders for the stones, destroyed by jealous pharaohs, or robbed of their treasures by thieves. Yet a picture of the Egyptian way of life has been pieced together by scholars who have carefully excavated buildings, examined mummies, and studied the inscriptions on walls and in papyrus scrolls.

True scientific research in Egypt dates from 1799, when scholars began the struggle to decipher the hieroglyphs on the Rosetta Stone. By 1822, as the Egyptian writing began to be understood, there was great interest in the ancient land. In the late 19th century, two large groups of mummies were found at Thebes. Among 33 royal coffins were those of Ahmose I, the founder of the New Kingdom, Thutmose III, and Ramses II. Centuries ago priests had removed the mummies from their original tombs and buried them in secret chambers to protect them from tomb robbers. X-ray examinations of the bodies revealed information about the Egyptian diet, their diseases and medical treatments, and their embalming methods.

The desert air of Egypt has preserved almost everything—mummies, papyrus, cloth, gold, and even wood. In 1954 the wooden funeral boat that carried the body of Cheops across the Nile to his pyramid at Giza was uncovered in almost perfect condition. In the 1960s two bodies were found at Saqqara in an Old Kingdom tomb. They had been preserved for 4500 years.

In Nubia, part of the New Kingdom empire, over 20 monuments have been rescued from the lake created by the building of the Aswan High Dam. The temples of Ramses II and his queen at Abu Simbel were cut into 30-ton blocks and moved to a site above the level of the new lake. But in a land so rich in ancient ruins, much of Nubia is now a drowned museum of temples and towns.

No discovery in Egypt has caused greater excitement than the opening of Tutankhamon's tomb in 1922. Yet now, over 50 years later, archeologists are still making startling discoveries, and the sands of Egypt may hold even more secrets.

Index